THE ULTIMATE ANIMAL LIBRARY
Raccoons
by Janie Scheffer
BLASTOFF! READERS
2
BELLWETHER MEDIA • MINNEAPOLIS, MN

Blastoff! Readers are carefully developed by literacy experts to build reading stamina and move students toward fluency by combining standards-based content with developmentally appropriate text.

Level 1 provides the most support through repetition of high-frequency words, light text, predictable sentence patterns, and strong visual support.

Level 2 offers early readers a bit more challenge through varied sentences, increased text load, and text-supportive special features.

Level 3 advances early-fluent readers toward fluency through increased text load, less reliance on photos, advancing concepts, longer sentences, and more complex special features.

★ **Blastoff! Universe**

Reading Level

Grade K

Grades 1–3

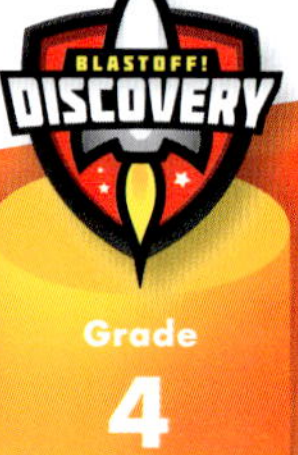

Grade 4

This edition first published in 2025 by Bellwether Media, Inc.

Library of Congress Cataloging-in-Publication Data

LC record for Raccoons available at: https://lccn.loc.gov/2024012125

Editor: Elizabeth Neuenfeldt Series Designer: Veah Demmin

Printed in the United States of America, North Mankato, MN.

Table of Contents

What Are Raccoons?

Raccoons are **mammals** with black markings around their eyes. They look like they are wearing a mask! They mostly live in North and Central America.

Raccoon Report

Range

Status in the Wild

least concern

Habitats

forests

grasslands

wetlands

Raccoons have fuzzy ears.
Their **snouts** are pointy.

tail

Their **bushy** tails can have many light and dark rings.

Raccoons are covered with grayish-brown fur.

Their fur colors help them hide in their **habitats**. They stay safe from **predators**.

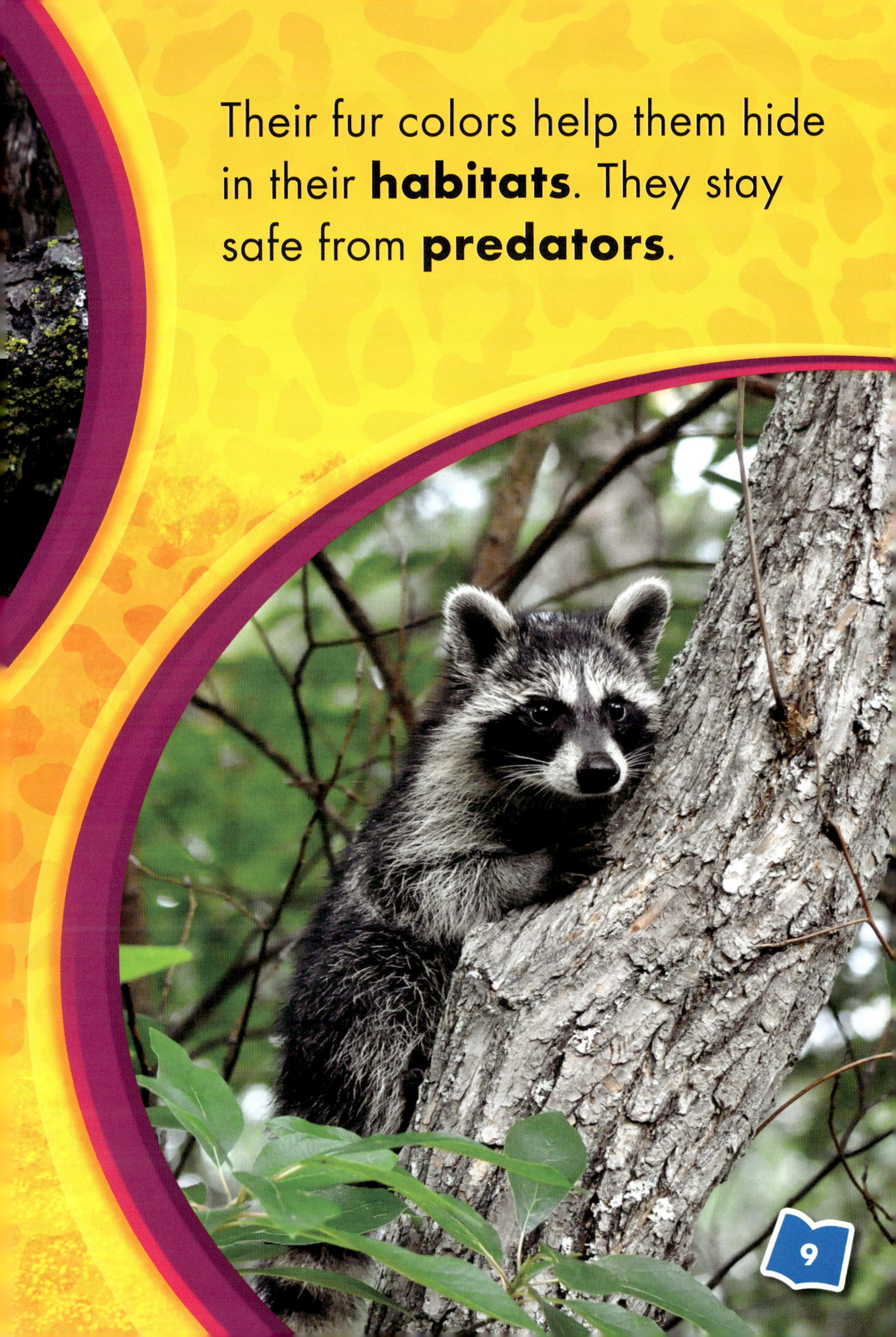

Raccoons have five toes on each foot. Their front toes move like fingers. Raccoons can hold food and open things.

Raccoons have strong claws. Their claws help them climb.

Spot a Raccoon
bushy tail
black markings around eyes
pointed snout

Good Eaters!

Many raccoons live in cities, forests, and **grasslands**. They sleep in **dens**. They mostly rest in trees or **burrows**.

They are **nocturnal**. But they can move around during the day.

Raccoons are **omnivores**. Their **diets** are based on where they live.

fruit

In cities, they eat food from trash cans. In the wild, they eat **insects**, mice, and fruit.

Raccoons often eat more in the spring and summer.

Raccoon Food Web

gray wolves
coyotes
great horned owls
insects
mice
fruit

In the winter, they mostly stay in their dens.

Growing Up

Female raccoons raise up to seven **cubs** at once.

The cubs stay in their dens for about two months.

cubs

Cubs stay close to their mothers.
Mothers teach cubs how to hunt.

Around one year later, cubs live on their own. They will begin their own families!

Glossary

burrows—tunnels or holes in the ground used as animals' homes

bushy—thick and fluffy

cubs—baby raccoons

dens—sheltered places

diets—the foods animals eat

grasslands—lands covered with grasses and other soft plants with few bushes or trees

habitats—places where animals live

insects—small animals with six legs and bodies divided into three parts

mammals—warm-blooded animals that have backbones and feed their young milk

nocturnal—active at night

omnivores—animals that eat both plants and animals

predators—animals that hunt other animals for food

snouts—the noses and mouths of some animals

To Learn More

AT THE LIBRARY

London, Martha. *Raccoons.* Lake Elmo, Minn.: Focus Readers, 2021.

Mattern, Joanne. *Raccoons.* Minneapolis, Minn.: Kaleidoscope, 2023.

Riggs, Kate. *Raccoons.* Mankato, Minn.: Creative Education and Creative Paperbacks, 2023.

ON THE WEB

FACTSURFER

Factsurfer.com gives you a safe, fun way to find more information.

1. Go to www.factsurfer.com.
2. Enter "raccoons" into the search box and click .
3. Select your book cover to see a list of related content.

Index

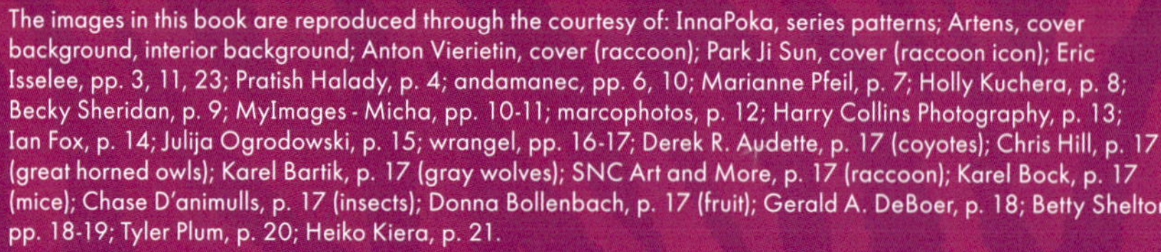

The images in this book are reproduced through the courtesy of: InnaPoka, series patterns; Artens, cover background, interior background; Anton Vierietin, cover (raccoon); Park Ji Sun, cover (raccoon icon); Eric Isselee, pp. 3, 11, 23; Pratish Halady, p. 4; andamanec, pp. 6, 10; Marianne Pfeil, p. 7; Holly Kuchera, p. 8; Becky Sheridan, p. 9; MyImages - Micha, pp. 10-11; marcophotos, p. 12; Harry Collins Photography, p. 13; Ian Fox, p. 14; Julija Ogrodowski, p. 15; wrangel, pp. 16-17; Derek R. Audette, p. 17 (coyotes); Chris Hill, p. 17 (great horned owls); Karel Bartik, p. 17 (gray wolves); SNC Art and More, p. 17 (raccoon); Karel Bock, p. 17 (mice); Chase D'animulls, p. 17 (insects); Donna Bollenbach, p. 17 (fruit); Gerald A. DeBoer, p. 18; Betty Shelton, pp. 18-19; Tyler Plum, p. 20; Heiko Kiera, p. 21.